GHOSTING THE PARTY
MELISSA BUBNIC

CURRENCY PRESS
The performing arts publisher

GRIFFIN THEATRE COMPANY

CURRENT THEATRE SERIES

First published in 2022
by Currency Press Pty Ltd,
PO Box 2287, Strawberry Hills, NSW, 2012, Australia
enquiries@currency.com.au
www.currency.com.au

in association with Griffin Theatre Company.

Copyright: *Ghosting the Party* © Melissa Bubnic, 2022.

COPYING FOR EDUCATIONAL PURPOSES

The Australian *Copyright Act 1968* [Act] allows a maximum of one chapter or 10% of this book, whichever is the greater, to be copied by any educational institution for its educational purposes provided that that educational institution [or the body that administers it] has given a remuneration notice to Copyright Agency (CA) under the Act.

For details of the CA licence for educational institutions contact CA, 11/66 Goulburn Street, Sydney, NSW, 2000; tel: within Australia 1800 066 844 toll free; outside Australia 61 2 9394 7600; fax: 61 2 9394 7601; email: info@copyright.com.au

COPYING FOR OTHER PURPOSES

Except as permitted under the Act, for example a fair dealing for the purposes of study, research, criticism or review, no part of this book may be reproduced, stored in a retrieval system, or transmitted in any form or by any means without prior written permission. All enquiries should be made to the publisher at the address above.

Any performance or public reading of *Ghosting the Party* is forbidden unless a licence has been received from the author or the author's agent. The purchase of this book in no way gives the purchaser the right to perform the play in public, whether by means of a staged production or a reading. All applications for public performance should be addressed to Cameron's Management, Locked Bag 848, Surry Hills, NSW 2010; info@cameronsmanagement.com.au; (02) 9319 7199.

Typeset by Brighton Gray for Currency Press.
Cover shows Jill McKay; image by Brett Boardman.

Currency Press acknowledges the Traditional Owners of the Country on which we live and work. We pay our respects to all Aboriginal and Torres Strait Islander Elders, past and present.

 A catalogue record for this book is available from the National Library of Australia

Contents

GHOSTING THE PARTY   1

Theatre Program at the end of the playtext

'Thou hast nor youth, nor age,
But, as it were, an after-dinner's sleep
Dreaming on both'

Measure for Measure, William Shakespeare

Ghosting the Party was first produced by Griffin Theatre Company at the SBW Stables Theatre, Sydney, on 6 May 2022, with the following cast:

DOROTHY	Jillian O'Dowd
GRACE	Belinda Giblin
SUZIE	Amy Hack

Director, Andrea James
Designer, Isabel Hudson
Lighting Designer, Verity Hampson
Composer and Sound Designer, Phil Downing
Stage Manager, Madelaine Osborn

Ghosting the Party was developed with the support of the National Theatre Studio.

CHARACTERS

DOROTHY, 57, a teacher
GRACE, 87, her mother
SUZIE, 34, her daughter

ERIC, 71, wears a Fedora inside
RITA, 59, Suzie's colleague and mentor

NOTES

A line with no full stop at the end of a speech indicates that the next speech follows on immediately.

The use of '/' marks the point that the next line should begin.

Each scene title is announced by one of the company.

This play went to press before the end of rehearsals and may differ from the play as performed.

1.

No-one ever came back but all reports indicate it's lovely
Brain aneurysm. In your sleep
Ooh, that's lovely that
You go to bed tired, so ready to sleep, and you just … keep resting
There's no pain and no fear
And that's dying
Lovely
Do you think you would dream? The last time you went to sleep, do you think you would dream?
And if so, what about?
Something lovely like flying or that you forgot to turn the iron off?
There's always something left undone
Scientists say that during sleep, cerebral spinal fluid is pumped around the brain, and flushes out waste products like a biological dishwasher
I like the thought of dying with a clean brain, like washing your clothes before you go on holiday, you're ready
Course you want to be found immediately
Oh, first thing in the morning definitely
You don't want to be lying about for weeks
Bloating
Blackening
Farting
Leaking
The malodours
The flies
Not so bad in the winter though
You might have left the heating on, you could be a stew by the time they find you
Not if you have a temperature-controlled thermostat—which you most definitely should have
You'd want your eyes closed
I worry if they're open and the rigor mortis is so far advanced that your eyes are too stiff to close and your lids break off in some paramedic's hands

It's terribly intimate, your eyelids in a stranger's hands
I suppose the paramedic is already kneeling in your fluids and general … miasma death waft
I mean, it can't get more intimate
And they are a professional
Drowning
Oh no that's the worst!
It's not apparently, it's panic at first because your instinct is to fight it so that's the whole thrashing and gasping business, then tearing and burning as your lungs fill with water but then you start losing consciousness and you're not fighting any more, you're calm and tranquil and light
I still prefer the brain aneurysm
We all prefer the brain aneurysm but we can't all be so lucky
Stroke
Stroke is good as long as it's massive and final. You don't want the littler ones where you survive but you're peeing on the left because the right side of your body is kaput
Have you seen what the brain looks like after a fatal stroke?
It's like a frog flattened by a brick
Carnage
It's like they took your brain out of your body and dropped it from a twelve-storey building, then scooped up what they could and poured it back into your skull
Heart attack then, a massive coronary
They can hurt though
They do hurt—shortness of breath, heartburn, tightening chest, sharp intense pain
And no control over the time and place, you understand
You could be in the bath
You could be having a bath and then your arm starts to cramp and in your panic, you trip over the side, and there you are, sprawled over the tiles and it's your last hour on earth, on your own, in pain, wishing you had sprung for under-floor heating when you had the chance
That's how my sister went. To think she used to iron her underpants and did she get hit by a bus? No. It's out cold on the bathroom floor, completely naked, her pressed underpants eternally out of reach
Shark attack, death by shark

Obviously you shit yourself if you see a Great White coming at you, jaws open, your life flashes as you stare down that beady eye of prehistoric determinism but the efficiency, my god, the efficiency of a Great White's bite force, it can chomp through one-point-eight tonnes in a single bite, it'd be over like that, so if it's a choice between cancer and a Great White shark, well—
Well, of course if it's shark versus cancer, shark wins
Of course
But when's the last time a Great White swam up the Maribyrnong?

2.

Dorothy's home.
GRACE, DOROTHY *and* SUZIE *wear black, having just been to a funeral.*
DOROTHY *eats cake.*
SUZIE *is distracted on her phone.*

Old age should burn and rave at close of day
DOROTHY: The flowers were nice, weren't they?
SUZIE: Lovely service.
DOROTHY: McCaffrey's aren't the cheapest you know. Over eighteen hundred bucks—just on flowers. Still, apparently that's what your aunt wanted. I suggested they go with Anderson & Son, who we used for Dad. We were happy with the service, weren't we, Mum? But you know how your aunt was—money no object.
SUZIE: I liked the music. I said I liked the music, Nan.

    GRACE *doesn't respond.*

DOROTHY: She was on *Australian Idol*. The lady who did the singing was on *Idol*, Mum. The talent show on telly.
SUZIE: Really?
DOROTHY: She was never actually on telly, she didn't get through, but she auditioned.

    Beat.

The priest spoke well, didn't he?
GRACE: Saw him do the exact same speech at Maureen's a few weeks ago. Just swapped out the names.

DOROTHY: Maureen who?
GRACE: Maureen who used to work at Vic Roads.
DOROTHY: Was she a big, tall lady?
GRACE: No.
DOROTHY: Blonde hair?
GRACE: No.
DOROTHY: Irish?
GRACE: No.
DOROTHY: Don't know her.
GRACE: Neither did I.
SUZIE: Then why did you go to her funeral?
GRACE: Because I thought I did know her. I thought it was Maureen, Red Greg's daughter, who played cricket with your father, remember him? Nose like a radish? And then half way through, I realise it's the wrong Maureen but they're serving sausage rolls so …
SUZIE: It was a lovely service, Nan. Really. Aunt Betsy would've been happy.
GRACE: She was never happy.
SUZIE: If she hadn't suffered from depression, she would've been happy.
GRACE: This funeral has been the highlight of my year and I didn't know anyone there. There was no-one there.
DOROTHY: We were there! Her children, her grandchildren, all the important people were there. Suzie came all the way from Montreal. Wasn't it good for Suzie to come all the way from Montreal, Mum?
SUZIE: I had to come. It was Aunt Betsy. And we don't have a big family—
DOROTHY: You could've waited until after the funeral to break up with Emil. Then he could've come. We needed the numbers.
GRACE: S'pose the trick is to snuff it first, get a nice full church. You leave it too late everyone's already dead and you've overspent on catering.

> *Suzie's phone beeps—she has a message.*
>
> *She responds.*
>
> DOROTHY *clocks this.*

DOROTHY: Andrew didn't look too good, did he?
GRACE: He shouldn't have been there.

DOROTHY: Jeff insisted. He didn't think his dad should miss it.
SUZIE: I can't believe that was Uncle Andrew. Didn't recognise him.
GRACE: It wasn't right. Him making a disgrace of himself. He would've been so ashamed.
DOROTHY: It's probably a blessing, his mind being gone. He would've been heartbroken otherwise.
GRACE: S'pose dignity is a luxury none of us can afford now. I'm wearing Velcro shoes for crying out loud.
DOROTHY: They're trendy Mum, I promise.
GRACE: Suzie?

> SUZIE *looks at* GRACE*'s shoes.*

SUZIE: I think what's most important is that you're comfortable.
GRACE: I look like an idiot.
DOROTHY: You do not.
GRACE: I hate them and I hate myself for wearing them.
SUZIE: I honestly didn't know him. You didn't tell me he was so … y'know.
GRACE: That's the point. It wasn't Andrew. It was a possession. His body used against his will. It was a spectacle. That business of wailing and shaking. Would you let me out like that, in public?
DOROTHY: We're lucky you still have your marbles.
GRACE: I'm sure that's what Andrew said … right until he lost them.
DOROTHY: Shut up, Mum, don't get morbid, have some cake.
GRACE: That's your solution to everything, Dot, stuff your face. I don't see being fat making you happy.
DOROTHY: I am happy, Mum.
GRACE: Don't be stupid, Dorothy.

> DOROTHY *stops eating.*

I never really liked Betsy, stuck-up cow, but she was … I remember the day she was born, spent most of my childhood trying to kill her. Daring her to climb higher than she was comfortable with, hoping for a fall. A sharp push off the roof. Or I'd hold her head down in the bath, a pillow over her sour little face.

> *Beat.*

Now there's no-one who knows me.

DOROTHY: We know you, Mum.
GRACE: You don't know what it feels like to be the last person left. Everyone's gone. My parents, your father, my brother, now my sister, all my friends. It's just me.
DOROTHY: But you're hardly alone. We're here.
GRACE: You've no idea what it's like to wake up and stare at the ceiling for four hours with no impulse to move, because why? What's left to do?
DOROTHY: That's your problem, Mum. You're so negative. Can't you be grateful for what you have? You're in reasonably good health and you're alive. That makes you luckier than most.
GRACE: That's your problem, Dot—your relentless positivity. You set the bar so damn low. A pot plant can be alive—I've as much interest in being alive as I do in being a Swiss Cheese monstera.
DOROTHY: Oh Suzie! Do you know who's got cancer? Suzie, remember Mrs Spencer? Suzie?

    SUZIE *is still busy on her phone.*

SUZIE: Hmm?
DOROTHY: Mrs Spencer? You had her in Grade Two?
SUZIE: Um ... no.
DOROTHY: You remember her! Brown curly hair? Terrible acne scars? Remember her?
SUZIE: Okay ... ?
DOROTHY: Liver cancer. Nothing more they can do, maybe a few months at most. Ran into her daughter at the shops and she told me.
SUZIE: Okay.
DOROTHY: You remember her!
SUZIE: I actually don't, Mum.
DOROTHY: But you liked her. She played the guitar? She taught you *Hotel California.* [*Singing*] Welcome to the Hotel California ...
SUZIE: Okay. And she has liver cancer. Okay.
GRACE: Your whole life everything's ahead of you. And then one day you realise it's all behind you. And you're just waiting to die. And it's the waiting that gets you. I have three types of pills for my heart, then I've got the ones for blood pressure, and cholesterol, my liver, and gout and arthritis and anaemia and why? What am I trying so hard to stay alive for?

DOROTHY: I don't know, Mum, me? Your granddaughter? Touch wood you'll be around a long time yet.
GRACE: God, I hope not. I was walking home from church after Maureen's funeral and I don't know what I did but I was lost. I didn't recognise where I was. How many times have I walked that route? Have you ever been really lost? It's ... Is this how it starts? Has it already started?
DOROTHY: That happens to everyone, Mum. You forget something you've always known. I forgot to put sugar in my strudel. I was making a strudel for the baking rota—
GRACE: Bugger the strudel, Dorothy, you're not listening! It's not the same as being five minutes from the house you've lived in for sixty-four years and not knowing the way home!

Beat.

DOROTHY: But you got home, Mum. That's all I meant. It's not the harbinger of doom, it's a ... blip. And everyone has blips.
GRACE: Each day there's something else I can't do. I can't tell you the last time I looked up at the sky, I get too dizzy, I can't look up anymore without falling over, besides, there's too much happening on the ground, cracks and holes in the footpath, and cars and bikes, and blisters on my feet I can't reach and shouldn't have because I got these stupid Velcro shoes made special and spent more than two hundred on them, and a tin of ravioli for dinner which I can't open because of my arthritis, so I go to bed hungry but hardly hungry because I never feel full anyway but so tired and I can't sleep because this leg burns and I'm eighty-seven years old and what am I holding on for? Why shouldn't I just get it over with, kill myself?
DOROTHY: Shut up, Mum.
SUZIE: How would you do it?
DOROTHY: Don't encourage her.
SUZIE: But she has a point. We spend all this effort trying to keep people alive without thinking through whether life is really worth it.
DOROTHY: And what effort are you spending?
SUZIE: I was using the collective 'we', people, the health system, society. I'm not sure I want to live much past eighty either. No offence, Nan, but you're hardly sucking the marrow out of life, are you?

DOROTHY: Suzie!
GRACE: That's exactly right, Suzie, exactly right.
SUZIE: I mean, those shoes for a start.
DOROTHY: We can't be sucking the marrow out of life every day, can we? Live each day like it's your last—what a stupid sentiment. You'd never get anything done. Why fix the shelf in the bathroom if you're going to be dead? Why sort out your rego? Why eat bran?
GRACE: I don't know whether you do it on purpose or you can't help being this dense.
SUZIE: If a lemon's gone mouldy, you don't pop it in the fridge and keep it for another seventeen years, do you?
DOROTHY: My mother is not a lemon. A teacher at school, her grandmother is ninety and she still swims a kilometre each morning.
GRACE: Oh piss on that! I'm not about to start running marathons to prove age is just a number, you're as young as you feel, it's all a state of mind. Bullshit! I'm old and I feel it.
SUZIE: Razor along the wrists? You've got to cut length ways. It's an amateur mistake to go across.
GRACE: I don't want blood. Too gruesome. Someone has to clean up after you—it's not considerate.
SUZIE: Drive to the beach. Hose in the exhaust pipe. You fall asleep looking at the ocean.
GRACE: I don't drive.
DOROTHY: Stop it, both of you, it's not funny so stop joking about it.
GRACE: If you've been captured by the enemy, you swallow cyanide, don't you?
SUZIE: Death before captivity.
GRACE: Exactly!
DOROTHY: But you haven't been captured by the enemy—
GRACE: And I don't want to be. Betsy was three years younger than me, Andrew's younger than me. I want to get out while I can still do it. Before the stroke, the dementia, the fall ... Just once, I'd like to do what I want. And what I really want, is to die.
DOROTHY: Alright, Mum, go kill yourself. Somehow we'll make do without your cheery disposition. I don't know, maybe I'll get a cavapoo.

    GRACE *glares at* DOROTHY *and leaves.*

SUZIE *is still on her phone, responding to an email.*
Do you have to do that?
SUZIE: What?
DOROTHY: You're meant to be here with us and you're so ... preoccupied.
SUZIE: You do understand, right, that I'm not actually on holiday? I may physically be here but I still have to do my job.
DOROTHY: I know it's not a holiday, it's a funeral, Suzie.
SUZIE: Which I have been at all day!
DOROTHY: And you've been on your phone all day!

SUZIE *puts her phone away.*

SUZIE: Sorry, one of my campaigns is about to launch and it's my baby so, y'know, I just want everything to be perfect.
DOROTHY: Thought we could talk.
SUZIE: Hm-hm.

Beat.

DOROTHY: We haven't really had a chance to talk.
SUZIE: We talk literally all the time.
DOROTHY: But you never tell me anything.
SUZIE: I don't know what you want to know. Nothing I give you satisfies.
DOROTHY: Because you haven't explained why you and Emil broke up!
SUZIE: Because people break up! Relationships don't work out and it's sad and that's it.
DOROTHY: And he wasn't seeing someone else?
SUZIE: No.
DOROTHY: Were you?
SUZIE: No.
DOROTHY: You wanted to get married, he didn't?
SUZIE: No.
DOROTHY: Did he want to get married?
SUZIE: Maybe I should just record all conversations and give them to you and then you could know that you know all there is to know.
DOROTHY: People don't break up after seven years for no reason.
SUZIE: We just weren't happy anymore, Mum. And we were only together because we were already together.

DOROTHY: What does that mean?
SUZIE: It means ... it was habit. We ate breakfast at the same places, and had the same conversations with the same people and I just didn't want to anymore.
DOROTHY: Everyone feels that way. That's normal.
SUZIE: Yeah, okay, well—
DOROTHY: You're thirty-four years old, Suzie. And unless you're not telling me something, you've broken up with a decent man for no real reason.
SUZIE: I know you liked him.
DOROTHY: He was so pleased that his new job had such a good paternity package. I thought this year you two would finally have a baby.
SUZIE: I'm sorry.
DOROTHY: How you feel now is not how you will always feel. What seems so important—friends, your job, even men—none of it lasts. The only love that really lasts is between parents and children. And when we're gone, where will your love come from?
SUZIE: I still have time, Mum. I can meet someone. Have a baby. More than one even. Emil doesn't represent my last chance at happiness, I promise.
DOROTHY: I hope that's true.

3.

Grace's home.

During the following text, GRACE *gets up on a chair, ties a rope to a ceiling beam, creates a noose, which she puts around her neck.*

Get into the boat this instant, you lazy loitering rogue
From the moment your mother kisses the first boo-boo better, we understand that pain carries with it the expectation of help, of recovery
Scraped knees
Period cramps
The emergency hysterectomy
There are traumas, yes
But also the hot water bottle
A cup of tea
Endone and a crisp but affordable Clare Valley Riesling, and of course, time
But aging is disease without cure

That is why it's so terrifying
Jean Amery, the essayist, before he topped himself in a Salzburg hotel room, compared aging with torture
You're the prisoner, locked in the cell
The policeman's fist explodes your face in a bloody pulp of bone and cartilage
And in that blow, you understand everything that is to come
And know with devastating certainty that no-one is coming to rescue you
The irony is that despite knowing, truly in-your-bones *knowing* that the torture only ends when you're a corpse
It's still bloody hard to kill yourself
Her mind's made up, Grace thinks
It's time, she thinks
If not now, when?
And yet
And yet
From the moment we're born, we do whatever we can to cling to life
To do what we have always done
Breathe
And breathe
However rational your reasons are
It's not easy to stop doing what you have always done

    GRACE *has the noose around her neck. Will she let herself fall?*

4.

A bar, Montreal.

SUZIE *and* RITA *are finishing their martinis.*

It's not that we have a short time to live, but that we waste so much of it

RITA: So you cried, big deal.
SUZIE: It is a big deal.
RITA: We need another martini.

    RITA *indicates to waiter that they'll have two more martinis.*

SUZIE: I feel sick.

RITA: Maybe some prawn balls too. I'm fucking famished.

SUZIE's phone rings.

She clocks the caller and puts it on silent.

SUZIE: Have you ever cried?

RITA: In the office? In front of people? Fuck no! But I'm a cunt, everyone says so.

SUZIE: It's so weak, it's so …

RITA: Female?

SUZIE: I know that's not a very feminist thing to say but women cannot cry. Ever. You don't promote criers.

RITA: You think you won't be made a director because you got teary?

SUZIE: We so nearly missed the CFIA deadline and I just … I don't know. It was some bizarre physiological response to stress, completely uncharacteristic. Of all the people I could've cried in front of, why did it have to be Steven Cunningham?

RITA: So he thinks you're a weak woman but that isn't the worst thing— it means he gets to feel strong. It could work for you.

SUZIE: Steven will block me, I know it. Tell me to hang tight for a couple of years, y'know, wait for the next opportunity—

RITA: Your generation is so fucking impatient. I was nearly fifty before I was made a director.

SUZIE: If I can't be extraordinary, then am I just like everyone else but without the stuff? You know, arguments about cat litter and Roger's behavioural issues?

RITA: Is Roger the cat?

SUZIE: Roger is a hypothetical construct—standing in for obligations, dependents—which I choose not to have because I'm running a different race.

RITA: But if you can't win, you don't want to run?

SUZIE: It's not even that I don't want to, it's more, I don't understand the point. Like you only climb Everest to reach the summit, not to … fuck about in the middle. If I told my mum this, she'd say something dumb, like, 'it's just a job, a job won't hug you back'. Do you think it's possible to be happy without a family?

RITA: The demands on your time, energy, the sleep deprivation, the financial burdens—it's shit. Especially for women.

SUZIE: So you've never regretted … ?
RITA: Not really, no. No more than I regret the other decisions I didn't make. Why didn't I become a marine biologist and study … algae blooms off the coast of Costa Rica? There are so many other lives I could've lived—that doesn't mean there's anything wrong with this one.
SUZIE: The only thing that makes me wonder is how certain everyone is that I'll be proved wrong. I'll end up horribly sad and alone. Is it terrible that I'm actually not that afraid of being alone? The idea of living just for me feels like relief.

> SUZIE's *phone vibrates—a call on silent.*
>
> SUZIE *clocks the number and hangs up.*

Jesus, Mum.
RITA: Parents have to believe that having kids is the most important thing you can do. My sister had a prolapsed womb after her third baby.
SUZIE: What is that?
RITA: Oh honey, you're so young. It's when your womb falls out of your vagina. Google it.

> SUZIE *Googles it and gasps in horror.*

SUZIE: Holy fuck, what is that?
RITA: Your pelvic floor muscles are stretched and torn in childbirth so your organs slip right out of you. Incontinence, pain, sexual dysfunction. Happens to like, fifty percent of women.
SUZIE: No!
RITA: So your body's fucked and you're depressed but you feel your life has meaning, I guess.
SUZIE: What gives your life meaning?

> RITA *is stumped.*

RITA: Maybe I don't need meaning because I'm happy.
SUZIE: What's happiness?
RITA: Doing exactly what I want. Like a third martini on a Thursday evening before dinner.
SUZIE: So happiness is about being selfish, doing what you want, and meaning is about being selfless, taking care of others—

RITA: Like the kid who destroyed your vagina.
SUZIE: [*uncertainly*] I think I'm happy.

> *The beep of a WhatsApp message.*
>
> SUZIE *checks her phone. She's stunned.*

RITA: Suzie?
SUZIE: It was a just a joke. I thought we were joking.
RITA: Suzie, what's wrong?
SUZIE: My grandmother tried to kill herself.

5.

Dorothy's home.

DOROTHY *eats dinner, while* GRACE *stares at her untouched food, a soft-boiled egg.*

Everything, even desire, stops stinging … eventually

DOROTHY: This will be fun. I promise you, we're going to have fun. And it's a big help to me, y'know, sharing expenses and so forth. I haven't said but, it's been hard since Kenneth left. Your pension and my income, well, I'm telling you, Mum, it'll be a big help. And I'm hardly ever home so you'll have the run of the place. I've got salsa on Mondays, zumba on Tuesdays, book club once a month on Wednesday and sometimes we do Spanish night with those friends I made in that Spanish class. We'll host here occasionally so you can join in, eat some queso.
GRACE: I don't see why I couldn't stay in my own home.
DOROTHY: You know why. You can't be trusted on your own—it's not safe.
GRACE: It's really my own damn business.
DOROTHY: It's not just your business though, is it, Mum? It affects other people but you don't seem to realise that. That would require you to think of other people.
GRACE: I didn't go through with it, did I?
DOROTHY: Why didn't you? What stopped you?
GRACE: Can't we just forget it? I'm a stupid old woman, forget it.
DOROTHY: No thought to how I would feel when I found you.
GRACE: Like day follows night, you have to make it about you.

DOROTHY: What's the big deal? Just my mother hanging from the ceiling fan.
GRACE: God I wish I had done it, spared myself your braying.
DOROTHY: Do you have any idea the shame I've felt, the guilt, the questions they asked me? 'Has your mother ever spoken about taking her own life?' And what could I say?
GRACE: I don't know what the surprise is all about. I told you I wanted to die. I was very clear.
DOROTHY: I never thought you'd actually do it!
GRACE: And I didn't so stop carrying on like a bloody pork chop!

Beat.

DOROTHY *makes an effort to compose herself.*

DOROTHY: I should've taken your feelings seriously and I didn't and I'm sorry. I'm sorry. Just thank God you … I would never have forgiven myself.

Beat.

But now we have this second chance. I'm excited by this new chapter in our relationship. Living together as adults, girlfriends even. Share secrets, get to know each other, get close to each other.
GRACE: What are you talking about? We are close, we have a wonderful relationship.
DOROTHY: Sure, Mum, wonderful. Except for the part where you'd rather kill yourself than be with me.
GRACE: Come off it, Dorothy, you don't actually want me here.
DOROTHY: I just paid three hundred dollars to get a handrail installed in the shower—
GRACE: You know I prefer baths—
DOROTHY: I want you here!
GRACE: Bullshit. You feel guilty and that's not my problem.
DOROTHY: Okay, Mum, fine, no-one loves you, no-one wants you, fine.

DOROTHY *fights to stop crying.*

GRACE: Oh God, you're not crying are you?
DOROTHY: Of course I'm not fucking crying.
GRACE: What's the matter with you then?
DOROTHY: Don't worry, Mum, forget it.

GRACE: I'd love to forget it but you're the one making a song and dance!
DOROTHY: Don't pretend you have the slightest interest in my life!
GRACE: I'm not one to pry, Dot. If you want to tell me something—
DOROTHY: It's not prying, it's … caring, for fuck's sakes!
GRACE: So now I don't care?
DOROTHY: You've never been good at this, Mum, okay? And I'm an idiot for thinking that you're going to change now.
GRACE: Change how? I don't know what you want me to do—
DOROTHY: Nothing! You don't have to do anything!

Beat.

GRACE: Is this because Kenneth left you? Because I told you not to marry him.
DOROTHY: Thank you, Mum, that's really helpful.
GRACE: I wasn't happy in my marriage either, Dorothy. Not that we talked about things like that then.
DOROTHY: We don't have to talk about it now.
GRACE: And I didn't mind because I thought maybe everyone was unhappy and there was no point making a fuss of it.
DOROTHY: If it's any consolation, Mum, I think Dad was pretty miserable too.
GRACE: But you felt sorry for him, marrying me. Not sorry for me marrying him.
DOROTHY: I'm sorry for everyone, alright? Dad and I just got on better is all. He was more sensitive than you. Like he could be broken. You've always seemed … strong.
GRACE: Women have to be stronger, Dorothy. We don't have the luxury of breaking, withdrawing to the shed to listen to records. Someone had to make dinner.

Beat.

At least your father was good-looking. Kenneth on the other hand …

GRACE *bursts out laughing.*

DOROTHY: Okay, Mum, well, I'm sorry, again, for not being as beautiful as you so my options weren't—
GRACE: When I met him the first time, I thought …

GRACE *is now really hysterically laughing.*

DOROTHY: So he has a weak chin—
GRACE: Dorothy, I've seen weak chins! The man has no chin! A complete absence of chin! It's just teeth sitting on a neck!

   GRACE *can't stop laughing.*

God, what a drip!
DOROTHY: See Mum? We are having fun. Or at least you are.
GRACE: He doesn't deserve tears, Dorothy, believe me. One day you'll realise that him leaving is the best thing that could've happened to you. Now he can get old and sick and it's someone else's problem. You've saved yourself ... as much as two decades worth of his biopsies, and procedures, and moaning.
DOROTHY: His kidneys aren't much chop. He might need dialysis in a few years.
GRACE: Brilliant! See?
DOROTHY: S'pose that'll be 'Janine's' job now. Ferrying him to treatment three times a week. The chinless wonder.

   And now GRACE *and* DOROTHY *both laugh and laugh.*

GRACE: Oh blast! I've pissed myself!
DOROTHY: Yeah. Me too.
GRACE: I prefer these pads.
DOROTHY: You feel drier don't you?

   Beat.

GRACE: If we knew at the beginning how it ends, would we do it differently?
DOROTHY: Why, Mum? How does it end?
GRACE: A lifetime and nothing to show for it but mistakes. Every bloody thing a mistake.
DOROTHY: Everything? What about me? Am I just another mistake?

   DOROTHY *expects* GRACE *to say 'no' ... but she doesn't.*

I read somewhere that our eyes are in front because we are supposed to look ahead, not back.

   GRACE *gives* DOROTHY *a contemptuous look.*

It means, Mum, if you make the effort, there can still be so much to look forward to!

GRACE: Don't be stupid, Dot. You're a divorced high school teacher living with her mother. Frankly, I don't know how you get up in the morning.
DOROTHY: How can you say that to me? Happiness is a choice, Mum. I'm happy.
GRACE: How could you possibly be happy? I don't understand you.
DOROTHY: I have friends, my ... health, my daughter—
GRACE: Friends die, Dot. Health goes. You never see your daughter. You think when you're decrepit she's moving you in? Ha, she's no mug. Trust me, Dot, no-one wants an old woman, no-one.

DOROTHY *is disturbed. Is* GRACE *telling the truth?*

6.

How sharper than a serpent's tooth it is to have a thankless child
Few insects parent their young
They normally drop a glop of eggs somewhere and that's parenting done
But the Japanese red bug is different
Their young nymphs are fussy eaters, they'll eat only one type of fruit from a rare tree
So their mother, wanting to please the little tykes, goes out and collects this one type of fruit from a rare tree
Searches for hours, probing and testing every fruit for ripeness
Rejecting one after the other
For hours, for literally hours
Fighting off other insects, would-be thieves (the fucking opportunists)
Crawling under and over ditches and debris, lugging this perfectly ripe, one type of fruit from a rare tree double her body weight
It's the Battle of the fucking Somme out there for the Japanese Red Bug mother and she does it, she keeps doing it
And the bigger her babes get, off the back of Mum's hard graft, the harder Mum needs to graft
Until all she's doing day and night is collecting the perfectly ripe, one type of fruit from a rare tree double her fucking body weight, so Mum works and works and they demand and demand more and more and more and she works and works and works until she's dead
And then they eat her
And that's parenting.

7.

Dorothy's home/Suzie's apartment.

DOROTHY *phones her daughter,* SUZIE, *in Canada.*

Love runs downhill

DOROTHY: Is everything alright?
SUZIE: Mum? What time is it there?
DOROTHY: Four thirty-six, seven.
SUZIE: In the morning?
DOROTHY: I can't sleep. Are you alright?
SUZIE: Are you alright?
DOROTHY: You haven't messaged me, you haven't called—
SUZIE: I message you all the time.
DOROTHY: Not since last week.
SUZIE: I've been busy—
DOROTHY: A little WhatsApp message. 'Hi Mum, how are you?' Just a few words. How busy can you be?

Beat.

SUZIE: I'm sorry, how are you?
DOROTHY: I can't sleep.
SUZIE: You said.

Beat.

Heard from Dad?
DOROTHY: Y'know we're not speaking.
SUZIE: Yeah, he said.
DOROTHY: When did you speak to him?

Beat.

SUZIE: I didn't—
DOROTHY: You spoke to him and you didn't tell me!
SUZIE: You're my favourite. I love you, I hate him.

Beat.

How's the house?

DOROTHY: How's the house? What d'you want to know about / the house for?
SUZIE: I dunno, nothing.

Beat.

DOROTHY: What's news?
SUZIE: God, Mum, I don't know. Nothing. I'm at work till nine most nights. What do you want me to tell you?
DOROTHY: Okay, you don't want to talk to me, fine.
SUZIE: I didn't say I don't want to talk to you, I just feel … God, it's like you want me to be interesting and entertain you and I'm not interesting and entertaining so I just feel I'm disappointing you.
DOROTHY: Come for Christmas.
SUZIE: What?
DOROTHY: Remember when you were little, your dad and his brothers, and I'd cook for days beforehand, and we'd have a house full of people, and kids running everywhere—
SUZIE: You were so stressed you'd cry, every year, without fail.
DOROTHY: But it was fun, Christmas day was fun.
SUZIE: I don't remember it being like that. You were stressed about everything. The food, the table, whether Oscar would have another epileptic fit and had you put your Lladró swan sufficiently out of reach—
DOROTHY: Yes, I'd cry beforehand and get angry with your father for being useless but all those people around a table—
SUZIE: And the fretting about the turkey—'Has it cooked? Is it dry? What's your father done with the thermometer?'
DOROTHY: Come home for Christmas.
SUZIE: Mum … I've just been home for the funeral.
DOROTHY: I'll pay for your flight.
SUZIE: I don't need you to, I have more money than you.
DOROTHY: So you can pay for it.
SUZIE: Mum—
DOROTHY: Suzie, I really need you to be home. Your grandmother is … I think she needs her family around her. I think she needs us.
SUZIE: What's wrong with her?
DOROTHY: She tried to kill herself, Suzie.
SUZIE: I know that but … is she okay now?

DOROTHY: She's depressed. She's on anti-depressants.
SUZIE: Everyone's on anti-depressants.
DOROTHY: Don't be flippant, everyone is not on anti-depressants. Are you on anti-depressants?
SUZIE: Citalopram. I've been on them for years.
DOROTHY: Why are you on anti-depressants?
SUZIE: Because I get depressed.
DOROTHY: Since when?
SUZIE: Since forever.
DOROTHY: But you've always been such a happy girl!
SUZIE: Okay.
DOROTHY: Okay, what?
SUZIE: I've always been happy ... except when I'm depressed.
DOROTHY: Why is everything a joke? This isn't funny.
SUZIE: I'm not joking. I'm seriously on anti-depressants because without them I get so fucking depressed I can't get out of bed and I fantasise all day about throwing myself in front of a train and then feeling guilty about the train driver feeling guilty and then thinking I'm such a selfish bitch, fuck the train driver. That is seriously the truth—no joke.

Beat.

DOROTHY: Why didn't you tell me?
SUZIE: Because I knew you'd make it about you and what you'd done, or should've done, when it has nothing to do with you and it's just the way it is.

Beat.

Mum, are you there?
DOROTHY: I wish you didn't have to grow up.
SUZIE: Mum, I'm actually really fine.
DOROTHY: I just wish I could hold you and you could stay small in my arms forever.
SUZIE: I don't think that would work for me so much.
DOROTHY: One day you'll understand this, how I feel, how it feels to love someone so much you—
SUZIE: I don't know, Mum, if I'm ever going to feel like—
DOROTHY: You will. You're still young, you still have time.
SUZIE: Yeah, yeah, I know.

DOROTHY: I'm so scared for you, how you—
SUZIE: Don't be. I'm happy.
DOROTHY: Then why are you on anti-depressants?
SUZIE: This is why I shouldn't have told you. Because you can't understand what you can't understand and you have no interest in trying—
DOROTHY: Regret is an awful awful thing Suzie, and I never want you to know what it feels like, this knot in your stomach and there isn't a moment you don't feel the loss of the decisions you didn't make—
SUZIE: Do you know what I'm going to do for Christmas, Mum? I'm going to a friend's house and we're going to knock over a few bottles of wine and a shitload of cigarettes and I couldn't give a fuck if the turkey is dry, moist, or even exists. Maybe I'm not going to wake up at forty, or fifty or a hundred and regret not living your life—maybe I don't want what you want.
DOROTHY: Do you think I want the wrong things? Is something wrong with me?
SUZIE: What are you talking about?
DOROTHY: Just something your grandmother said about mistakes ... should I have done things differently?
SUZIE: I think you should have done everything differently—but then I would, because I'm different from you. Why? Do you think you should have done things differently?
DOROTHY: I don't know what else I could have done.
SUZIE: Maybe you're living the life that's right for you.
DOROTHY: In the life I imagined, your father didn't leave me for his podiatrist. I thought I'd end up more at the centre of things instead of on the edges of everyone else's lives.
SUZIE: Do you have a prolapse?
DOROTHY: What?
SUZIE: I just found out that it's a thing. Do you?
DOROTHY: A stage two bladder prolapse and a stage one rectal prolapse. Why?
SUZIE: Are you incontinent?
DOROTHY: Only when I sneeze. Or cough. Or laugh.

Beat.

SUZIE: What will you do for Christmas?

DOROTHY: I won't bother with the whole turkey business if it's just the two of us. Might pop a couple of chicken breasts in the oven. Bit of rosemary.

Beat.

Tarragon maybe.

SUZIE: Tarragon's nice.

DOROTHY: I won't do a Christmas tree. It's a lot of work y'know, the tree, and the decorations, and pudding—

SUZIE: You always make pudding. You always take a photo of the pudding all lit up. It's essentially the same photo every year but you—

DOROTHY: I'll just buy ice cream. There's this nice brand—I wish I could remember the name. Hoo me? Moo me? Tang me? Something like that. It's got a picture of a cow on the front. And pecans.

SUZIE: Pecans are nice.

Beat.

DOROTHY: I like almonds too.

SUZIE: M-hmm.

DOROTHY: How do you feel about the Brazil nut?

SUZIE: How do you feel about the Brazil nut?

DOROTHY: There's a lot of nut to them, but I don't find the flavour to be that interesting.

Beat.

SUZIE: I'm sorry I can't be there. For Christmas.

DOROTHY: If you can't, you can't.

SUZIE: And I'm sorry Nan's depressed.

DOROTHY: She's never really been a 'glass half full' kind of person

SUZIE: And I'm sorry I haven't WhatsApped more. We're doing a huge restructure, laying off half the company, I don't know where I'm going to end up, I might be promoted, or side lined or … and now is such an incredibly busy time to—

DOROTHY: You're never coming home, are you?

SUZIE: Next Christmas I'll—

DOROTHY: I mean to live. Since you and Emil are no longer … I thought you might … but you're not going to.

Beat.

SUZIE: Probably not, no.
>   *Beat.*

DOROTHY: If you come next Christmas, I'll definitely make pudding.
SUZIE: You know I hate Christmas pudding.
DOROTHY: But we'll get a photo of you, with the pudding, all lit up.
>   *Beat.*

>   Is it snowing there?

SUZIE: Yes.
DOROTHY: Yes, I know, saw it on the internet. I follow the weather in Montreal so I know what you see out the window.

8.

She gazes into the quag of her past like a gypsy into the crystal of the future
There's a way of seeing yourself
Which may bear no relation to what others see when they look at you
But it's the you that exists in your mind, the way you think you look, the way you think you are
It's why you're surprised when you're not very attractive in photos
Because the you that exists in your mind, well, your nose is straighter, your hair has more volume, your nipples aren't observable in that blouse
And this you that exists in your mind changes as you change, it has to, because there are many different versions of you over a lifetime
There's the you at eight, who rollerskates and chews your hair into disgusting wet clumps
There's the you at sixteen, you're overweight, you've got acne, you're desperately in love with Derek Fitzgerald but he regards you as one would the pus from a burst blackhead
There's the you at thirty-one, you're still overweight but you hide the acne scars behind a sebum-inhibiting matt foundation, you even have sex occasionally with your husband and don't really mind that the question of your orgasm is never considered
There's the you at fifty-seven, your ex has remarried and he's happy and publicly you're happy he's happy but privately you think he's a cunt, because the closest you get to intimacy is your pap smear and you

don't even care who does it because lying on your back with your eyes closed you could almost cry with relief because you're so lonely and this stranger's gloved fingers brushing against your vulva is the first time you've been touched by another human being in months
And so on and so on, the different versions of you over a lifetime
You change but you're still the same person, there's still some essence of you in every version, the you-ness of you is still you
But sometimes the person you see in the mirror is so different from the you that exists in your mind that they bear no relationship to each other at all
And the person looking back at you is an alien
You touch your face and you're shocked that the alien touches her face also
The skin beneath your fingers feels like tissue paper, the creases of unfolded origami
Where did you go?
Where did your you-ness disappear to?

9.

A restaurant.

DOROTHY *is on a date with* ERIC.

ERIC *wears a tight-fitting Fedora.*

The tragedy of growing old is not that you are old, but young
DOROTHY: This looks … nice.
ERIC: Yes, I've got a coupon, that's why I suggested we come here.
DOROTHY: Perhaps I'll have the chicken. I do like marjoram.
ERIC: The coupon's only good if you order from the fixed menu.
DOROTHY: Spaghetti Bolognaise then.
ERIC: But you get a garden salad. It includes a garden salad.
DOROTHY: Who doesn't like salad?
ERIC: Are you being funny?
DOROTHY: Pardon?
ERIC: I sometimes can't always tell if people are being funny.
DOROTHY: I just meant I like salad.
ERIC: You get a glass of wine too. Red or white?
DOROTHY: I'll have white.
ERIC: Red really would be better, with the spaghetti.

DOROTHY: Okay.
ERIC: So red or white?
DOROTHY: Red then.
ERIC: I like to get the selection out of the way first, I find it frees up the conversation.

> DOROTHY *nods.*

Otherwise we have our heads buried in the menus, and that impedes the conversation.

> DOROTHY *nods.*
>
> *Beat.*

And I always do the fixed menu when I come here, so that helps. I'm a man who knows what he wants.
DOROTHY: So it's good then? The Spaghetti Bolognaise?
ERIC: Not particularly but it's the best value, because it comes with the salad—
DOROTHY: The garden salad, yes.
ERIC: And the complimentary glass of wine. Though obviously it's not really complimentary because they've already included it in the price but they want us to think we're getting it for nothing but no-one's pulling the wool over my eyes. Still, at eight ninety-five for food and drink, you can't beat it, can you?

> ERIC *is sweating profusely. He wipes the sweat from his eyes.*

DOROTHY: Are you okay? You seem a bit … hot.
ERIC: Never better.
DOROTHY: Your hat maybe is a bit tight. Perhaps if you took your hat off?
ERIC: I'm fine.
DOROTHY: You're sweating into your eyes.
ERIC: No I'm not.

> ERIC *is blinking madly.*

DOROTHY: So your profile said you play badminton. Is that with a league or a club … ?
ERIC: My wife and I played. Before she died.
DOROTHY: Couldn't very well play *after* she died.

> DOROTHY *laughs, but* ERIC *doesn't.*

ERIC: Forty-seven years we were married.
DOROTHY: I'm so sorry.
ERIC: She had a remarkable backhand volley. Great feeling at the net. I called her The Meringue—such a light touch.
DOROTHY: Forty-seven years?
ERIC: For forty-seven years, every day's the same and then one day it's not.
DOROTHY: You said you were fifty-nine.
ERIC: Sorry?
DOROTHY: If you were married for forty-seven years, and you're fifty-nine, that means you got married when you were twelve.

Beat.

ERIC: I'm not following?
DOROTHY: It's okay not to be fifty-nine, and I knew that when I sat down, because I can … see—
ERIC: Are you trying to insinuate that I'm a liar? Me? When you clicked 'curvy' when, well … look at you!
DOROTHY: Why don't you take off your hat?
ERIC: What's my hat got to do with it?
DOROTHY: Because you're bald, and you're at least seventy and it's fine to be bald and seventy but don't wear a Fedora and don't say you're fifty-nine!

Beat.

ERIC *takes off his Fedora; he is bald.*

ERIC: If I admitted I was older, you wouldn't have agreed to a date.
DOROTHY: I'm sorry Eric but there's no point dating someone much past sixty. I know this sounds awful but how many good years could you possibly have left? One? Two? And that leaves me playing nurse to broken hips and dementia and if it comes to that I'd really rather die alone and spare myself the martyrdom. I'm so sorry, I know that's awful.

Beat.

But I mean, we're eating dinner at five p.m!
ERIC: We have to eat before six for the—
DOROTHY: The coupon, yes.

Beat.

ERIC: I'm sorry, on account of me being so old. There aren't a lot of women my age looking for love.
DOROTHY: I'm not exactly beating them back with a stick either.
ERIC: Are you going to leave?
DOROTHY: It took me an hour to get here and I am hungry, so—
ERIC: And it's very good value.
DOROTHY: It's excellent value.
ERIC: Good. Because the coupon is a two for one, so it won't work if I don't order two meals.
DOROTHY: Fine. But I'm having white wine.
ERIC: Red really would be—
DOROTHY: [*warning*] Eric.
ERIC: You're very attractive, Dorothy.
DOROTHY: I'm fat.
ERIC: Not in an unpleasant way.

Beat.

I miss it. Love.
DOROTHY: Me too.

10.

Dorothy's home.

During the following text, GRACE *pulls down her underpants and sits on the toilet.*

The Fall
A snowball rolls down a snow-covered hillside
As it rolls, the ball picks up more snow
Gaining more mass and surface area
Which means it picks up even more snow
Becoming larger and larger
This is called the Snowball Effect
A process that starts with something small
But builds upon itself, becoming larger
Graver
More serious
Disastrous

A process as inevitable and unstoppable as gravity
In the seconds after Grace completes her number two, and before her head connects with the marble effect floor her daughter thinks is sophisticated but really is a bit much
In the seconds before her seventh, eighth and ninth ribs break
In the seconds before the anterior cruciate ligament in her left knee tears Grace thinks that getting off the toilet isn't about getting off the toilet anymore
But about life
And how it has completely rolled away from her

> GRACE *falls off the toilet and onto the floor.*

GRACE: [*calling out*] Dot! Dot!

11.

Dorothy's home.
DOROTHY *is making* GRACE *comfortable, propping up her left leg.*

We cannot be created for this sort of suffering

DOROTHY: So a carer will come in and help us three times a day. I've told them that we want the same person each time but they can't promise that. I have said … it probably won't be the same person each time. It will most likely be different people each time, really interesting people though, all kinds, from all over—please don't be racist. I think it's a good thing, actually. It's company, chat. It'll be good for us. Meet new people. Stimulate the brain.

GRACE: I don't want them taking off my clothes.

DOROTHY: I can't change you on my own, Mum.

GRACE: I'll hold it.

DOROTHY: All day? You won't wee or poo for the entire day?

GRACE: I won't eat or drink anything. Nothing in, nothing out.

DOROTHY: That is not a realistic plan.

GRACE: You're not listening to me, Dorothy. I will not have some fleshy armed care assistant handling me. I will not.

DOROTHY: When you've recovered, and are walking again, you can use the toilet as normal. This is only temporary. Now let's do your physio.

GRACE: I don't want to.

DOROTHY: You need to do these exercises three times a day.
GRACE: You're actually enjoying this.
DOROTHY: What exactly am I enjoying, Mum?
GRACE: Dorothy's little invalid. Like rolling down my pantyhose and watching me shit is some kind of birthday treat.
DOROTHY: That's incredibly unfair.
GRACE: If anything, me falling off the bog has made you positively shine.
DOROTHY: I am grateful, Mum, that your injuries aren't more serious. I am grateful that work has given me time off to look after you. I am grateful that I can help.
GRACE: See? You're radiant! It's disgusting.
DOROTHY: Let's go, right leg. Glide your heel towards your bottom.
GRACE: I'm tired, Dorothy.
DOROTHY: You can't expect to get better if you won't put in the work.

Beat.

Alright, but tomorrow no excuses.
GRACE: No, Dorothy. I mean really tired.

Beat.

DOROTHY: I better get started on that salmon. It's a day overdue, if we don't use it tonight, we'll have to throw it out. Do you want me to put the telly on?
GRACE: Dot, please. This is not what I want. It's why I should've … but I was too gutless I couldn't then but now, it's actually here. And I'm scared, Dot, please. I can't bear it, I can't. I've lived my life, Dot. It may not have been the best life but it was mine. But now it's … we both know the direction of travel from here. It only gets worse. I will not become Betsy or Andrew or your father, everyone looking at the ceiling, staring at their lap, never at them, wishing they'd just die already but no-one having the courage to end it. I wish to God I could do it myself, Dot, but I can't even get out of this bed. I need your help. Please, I'm begging you, please. Let me go.

Beat.

Dot?

12.

A bar, Montreal.

SUZIE *is with* RITA *and they've had one round of martinis.*

Worms feed on Hector brave and Hector weak the same

SUZIE: I'm sorry, I really am.
RITA: Why? You got what you wanted. Congratulations. You're the youngest director ever at Goldacre Holt Vogl. Do you get a parade?
SUZIE: I know it seems bleak right now but with time I think—
RITA: Are you taking my office?
SUZIE: No-one's given any thought to—
RITA: It's twice the size of your office. Of course you're going to take it. You're not an idiot.
SUZIE: I want you to know I did fight for you. Not just because I like you, respect you, but because I think the business case is there—it's short termist to dump our consumer offer.
RITA: Am I supposed to be grateful that you fought for me?
SUZIE: I just … wanted you to know.
RITA: I've been at this company for twenty-four years and they fuck me a year out from my long-service entitlements. And they send my fucking protégé to complete the assassination. I hired you.
SUZIE: I know—
RITA: I looked after you—
SUZIE: I know—
RITA: Don't tell me what you know! I couldn't give a shit what you think you know! I can't even remember how many restructures I've survived but they get you in the end I guess, they come for everyone in the end. Not you, right? You think this could never happen to you. You'll never be in this position, you'll never become a 'savings opportunity'. I know you think that because it's what I thought. That's the thing, young people can't imagine what it is to be old and on the scrap heap, but we fucking remember what it is to be you.
SUZIE: What will you do?
RITA: I'm fifty-nine years old. I'm more likely to be fucked by a unicorn than get another job.

SUZIE: That's not true—
RITA: No-one will give me a job at this salary, and I'm too old and experienced to be paid less. Besides, no-one wants to manage their mother—it's embarrassing for everyone.
SUZIE: Let's get another martini, come on, my round.
RITA: I don't think so.
SUZIE: Maybe next week we could get together?
RITA: What for?
SUZIE: Well … I don't know, just … catching up.
RITA: You think we're friends?

Beat.

We worked together for ten years—
SUZIE: Twelve—
RITA: And now we don't. There's no reason for us to ever see each other again.
SUZIE: I really don't want this to be our last conversation.
RITA: I don't care what you want. I'm not your fucking mother.

RITA leaves a distressed SUZIE alone.

13.

Dorothy's home.
GRACE still has her left leg propped up.
A tray of untouched food beside her.
DOROTHY and SUZIE are with her.
The three have been silent for some time.

I shall leap from a building that is crumbling and tottering

SUZIE: Are we just not going to talk about it?
DOROTHY: I've nothing left to say to her.
GRACE: If only that were true.
DOROTHY: Don't think I haven't been tempted to kill her myself.
GRACE: Promises, promises.
DOROTHY: You talk to her because I can't be trusted not to say something awful.
GRACE: Little Miss Positive's struggling a bit.

DOROTHY: You're a fucking witch!
SUZIE: Mum!
DOROTHY: Sorry, sorry.
SUZIE: Nan, maybe you could ... Mum's really trying.
GRACE: Who asked her to?
SUZIE: You have to eat, Nan.
GRACE: Not hungry.
SUZIE: Yeah, but ... you have to.

GRACE shakes her head.

You really can't afford to lose any more weight. Those cheekbones are so prominent they're about to pierce skin.
DOROTHY: I've told her all this. Starvation is ugly, Mum. You'll look terrible in the casket.
GRACE: You'll make sure I'm presentable, won't you, Suzie? Not the make-up artist who did Betsy, so orange and all that blush—
SUZIE: Nan, this can't be what you want. Starving to death, it's ... horrific. We're talking weeks, long, drawn-out, the worst possible end.
GRACE: I'd much rather put a bag over my head and be efficient but Caesar over there is so damn unreasonable.
DOROTHY: You're too bloody strong. You should take that as a sign— you're not ready to die.
GRACE: A sign? From who?
DOROTHY: I don't know, God, or the universe or something.
GRACE: God? I've as much time for him as I do the Easter Bunny. God? Don't make me laugh.
SUZIE: You don't believe in God? Since when?
GRACE: Do you believe in God?
SUZIE: Of course I don't.
GRACE: The meek shall inherit the earth? Ha. What a con.
SUZIE: I can't believe you don't believe in God.
GRACE: You understand me, don't you, Suzie? You're not upset with me?
SUZIE: No.
GRACE: Because I don't want to normalise suicide. That's what your mother says I'm doing, normalising suicide.
SUZIE: Right.
GRACE: I really like you, Suzie. You've got something.

SUZIE: What have I got?
GRACE: Spirit. You've got spirit. I've no idea where you got it from but you've got it. You hold onto that. Everyone will want to take it away from you, but don't you let them.
SUZIE: Thanks, Nan.

> SUZIE *and* GRACE *hug.*
>
> DOROTHY *is incensed.*

DOROTHY: [*to* GRACE] Why are you so nice to her and such a bitch to me? Where are my hugs?
GRACE: You annoy me.
DOROTHY: You know I'm the only one who actually loves you? It doesn't matter to Suzie whether you live or die.
SUZIE: Of course it matters to me—
DOROTHY: Yes, yes, it matters but it doesn't *matter*. It makes no real difference to your life at all. I'm the one who's here. Who's always been here.
GRACE: Christ, I know.
DOROTHY: Why don't we all just kill ourselves then? Have a great, big suicide party!
GRACE: Oh God, the theatrics!
SUZIE: Everyone's lost their fucking mind.
DOROTHY: What have I got to live for? I'm fat, I'm old, I've been dumped. You think there aren't days when I'm watching some awful home renovation show picking Dorito crumbs out of my cleavage that I don't wonder what the hell is the point? So why shouldn't I kill myself?
GRACE: I didn't care for your tantrums as a child and it's even less attractive now.
DOROTHY: You didn't answer, Mum. If it's okay for you to die, why isn't it okay for me?
SUZIE: Mum …
GRACE: Don't be stupid, Dot.
DOROTHY: Dr Rahman thinks we should try electroconvulsive therapy.
SUZIE: Shock therapy? Do they still do that?
GRACE: You can't be serious—
DOROTHY: It's not as bad as you think. You don't feel a thing, you're under general anaesthetic. You wake up and maybe you feel disoriented,

a little confused but that's only short term. The hope is longer term, the electric charge to your brain will trigger you out of your depression.
GRACE: Absolutely not—
DOROTHY: An appointment's been made for the day after next.
GRACE: This is still my life, Dorothy! You can't—
DOROTHY: I have power of attorney. I can. And if you fight me, I'll have you declared mentally incompetent.
GRACE: I am not mentally incompetent—
DOROTHY: So eat!
GRACE: No!
DOROTHY: You are suffering from serious depression and therefore lack capacity to make choices about your care. So I have to do it for you. Dr Rahman agrees with me, Dr Lynskey, and your GP—
GRACE: You spiteful, selfish bitch!
DOROTHY: And if the ECT doesn't work, and you still won't eat, you'll be admitted to hospital and fed intravenously.
GRACE: It's pathetic. You're pathetic. Keeping me around like some fucking pet rock, just so you have someone to look after, because you're lonely, to give your pathetic little life a point.
DOROTHY: It may be pathetic, Mum, but it's my life and you're not taking it from me.
GRACE: I wish you were never born!
DOROTHY: They can tie you to the bed if they need to so you can't rip out the tubes!

GRACE *flings the tray of food to the floor, startling everyone.*

GRACE: You are not my daughter. I hate you, I hate you!

A horrible silence.

SUZIE: Mum, you don't want to do this.
DOROTHY: It's not easy doing the right thing.
SUZIE: Yeah, but right for who?
DOROTHY: For everyone!
SUZIE: Okay but—
DOROTHY: Why are you taking her side?
SUZIE: I'm not taking sides—
DOROTHY: You are! You're ganging up on me and then you'll both piss off and leave me holding the fucking bag.

SUZIE: What bag? What are we talking about?

DOROTHY: What's wrong with me? What did I do to make everyone leave?

SUZIE: I didn't leave you I—

DOROTHY: You were moving to Canada just for a year, remember? Just for an adventure. Then you might as well stay until your visa ran out. Then you met Emil. Why are you still there?

SUZIE: Because I'm … I'm happy, I—

DOROTHY: But your family is here! Don't you understand that I'm getting older and there'll be a time when you come back for your once-a-year visit and I won't remember you? If you have kids I won't know them!

Beat.

SUZIE: Well, I'm not having kids so—

DOROTHY: You say that now—

SUZIE: No, I mean it—

DOROTHY: I just hope to God you haven't left it too late—

SUZIE: I had an abortion. End of last year. Emil wanted it, but I didn't. I don't.

Beat.

And for all your warnings about not missing the boat on motherhood, if I'm going to be really honest, I don't know how happy being a mother makes you. At least, I just feel I'm always disappointing you. I'm not what you want.

DOROTHY: That's not true. I'm not what you want.

SUZIE: What do you think I want?

DOROTHY: You've always been ashamed of me! At sports day you told Jessica Mercurio I was your neighbour, a nice enough lady but boring as batshit. And you both laughed at my culottes. I heard you.

SUZIE: I don't remember—

DOROTHY: I heard you. I never said but I heard you. And you were with me when I bought those culottes and you said they looked nice!

SUZIE: Jesus, Mum, I was a kid! I'm so sick of … argh! You're like a ninja at emotional blackmail, always making me feel like everything I say or do impacts on your happiness. Why don't you just live your own fucking life?

DOROTHY: Because I didn't realise I was supposed to! I put you at the centre of my world because that's where I thought you belonged. And I shouldn't be surprised that you don't want to care for anyone else because all I ever taught you was how to take. So don't feel bad, I'm the one who made you an ungrateful little shit.
SUZIE: Why do you think I live ten thousand miles away? Because you're suffocating!
DOROTHY: You're right not to have children, you'd probably eat them!
GRACE: This is what she does. She hoards grievances and spits out a tsunami of venom when it suits. The things I could say if I had a mind to—
DOROTHY: Say it! Go on, say it!
GRACE: All this self-pitying rubbish about how no-one wants you. God give me strength.
DOROTHY: Do you know why I married Kenneth? Because I couldn't wait to move out of your house, to get away from you with your nit-picking and criticism and 'stay off the butter, Dorothy'. My whole life you've made me feel like a fat disappointment. No wonder Dad didn't love you. Because you're un-fucking-lovable! You're mean and rude and frankly, most of the time you're fucking horrible and if there was any justice in this world, it would've been you who got vascular dementia instead of Dad and died that horrible horrible death because he was a good man and you are an awful person with an ugly soul!

Beat.

GRACE: I did try to make your father love me. Be more ... what I thought he wanted. I got my hair done like Dusty Springfield (of course, we didn't know she was a lesbian then), and I made myself Brigitte Bardot eyes and I thought ... well, I mean I probably looked like a badger 'cause I couldn't wear my specs while I was doing it, you know, but I thought ... I thought I'd done rather well. His face, when he came home and saw me. I'd made a *Women's Day* pork roast with gravy to surprise him because we didn't have meat on a Wednesday and with my hair and eyes and in my blue dress—it was a Fletchers' blue dress above the knee, slit up the side ... And his face. The poor man didn't want me. What can you do? Wasn't his fault. He wasn't bad. Never hit me. Never counted my money—your father wasn't cheap, Dorothy. He wasn't unreasonable. He just didn't love me ... not like that.

SUZIE: Did you ever think maybe he didn't … like women, like that?
GRACE: Gay? Oh I don't know, Suzie. He had no sense of fashion.
SUZIE: That's not really evidence one way or the other.
GRACE: I married your father, Dorothy, when I was nineteen and you didn't come until I was thirty. And all those years I cried because I wanted you so much. So when you came, I felt so … I'd dress you up sweet, and people smiled at me in the street and I remember thinking, I'm grown up, I've done it, I made this, all this … this promise. That's why people want babies—because the future's not written. There's still a chance, you think, that … maybe it'll be different this time. And you think I don't love you? Don't be a goose, Dot, don't you know I would've been lost without you, that you're my miracle?

Beat.

DOROTHY: I'm so sorry, Mum, I didn't mean—
GRACE: Yes, you did. It's okay. We can say these things. Mothers, daughters, we hate each other, we love each other—it's what makes us special.

DOROTHY *laughs/cries, takes her mother's hand.*

DOROTHY: I don't know how you do it, it's really hard being mean.
GRACE: Don't sell yourself short, you were wonderfully cruel.

GRACE *kisses* DOROTHY's *hand.*

You're not the doormat you think you are, Dorothy.

SUZIE *hugs* DOROTHY.

SUZIE: I'm sorry what I said about the culottes.

DOROTHY *laughs/cries harder.*

DOROTHY: I'm sorry for making you feel like …
SUZIE: Same.

The three women hold each other in silence.

DOROTHY: You're not unloveable, Mum, you're really not. I'm sorry Dad was … how he was.
GRACE: I've never told a soul this … I slept with Rich Babinski.

Beat.

DOROTHY: What?
GRACE: With Rich. Just a few times. Before he died, we slept together.
DOROTHY: You don't mean … what do you mean? Exactly?
GRACE: I know it's been a while, Dorothy, but you do remember intercourse.
SUZIE: Nan, you slut.
GRACE: He loved me.
DOROTHY: I'm sure he said all kinds of things—
GRACE: No, Dorothy—he loved me. *Me.*
SUZIE: Was the sex any good?
GRACE: Not really but the attention was … nice. I mean, he was a toad but actually sort of sweet.
DOROTHY: Okay, well that's … good then.
GRACE: So you're not mad?
DOROTHY: I don't think any of that matters anymore, Mum.
GRACE: No, s'pose not.

14.

Dorothy's home.
DOROTHY *hands* GRACE *a bottle of pills and a glass of water.*
GRACE *swallows several pills.*

No-one, not the wise, nor the good, nor even the wild men has ever done enough to be ready to die
Mice taught to avoid the smell of cherry blossom passed on this phobia, this anxiety about cherry blossom to their children, and their grandchildren
So baby mice that have never experienced the scent of cherry blossom in their lives are extremely sensitive to it, because of the experience of their grandparents or even great grandparents
A parent's experience, even before conceiving, markedly influences the structure and function in the nervous system of subsequent generations
So we pass on memories
Which is a frightening thought when you think about it, the idea that trauma, anxiety, fear never dies but lives on in the next generation and the next

Do we ever escape the person our families make us?
Even when we react against them, we're only ever counterpoint to their lead melody
Women know this, we're under less illusion that our life is our own
It's a cliché that women are carers
But we are
We care for children, we care for parents, we care for friends, we care about dinner on the table and wiping the bench clean, we care about birthday cards and remembering the names of our kids' friends and teachers and karate classes, we care about anniversary parties and there being enough tonic in the fridge and taking Mum to her oncologist appointment, we care about the cat's annual vaccinations and getting the windows cleaned because they are fucking filthy, we care about ironing school dresses and going easy on the smoked paprika because Dad gets heartburn, we care and we care and we care
But the myth is that we love doing it, we love caring
When the truth is that it's what our DNA has been hardwired to do for generations
Caring is a burden
Love is a burden
It's work that never ends
And we wish to God someone else would do the caring and the loving because then maybe we could just rest
Because no matter how much you care, it's never enough, it's always what else do I need to fix? What more could I have done? Did I do enough and the answer is never yes
Men get to be the lead characters in their own narrative, but women don't have the time to make their stories, they have too much unfinished business
Few women can say enough now, I have loved and cared enough

> GRACE *is now asleep.*
>
> DOROTHY *gently places a plastic bag over her head, ties it firmly.*
>
> *She and* SUZIE *hold* GRACE*'s hands as they watch the bag inflate and deflate with* GRACE*'s breath.*

THE END

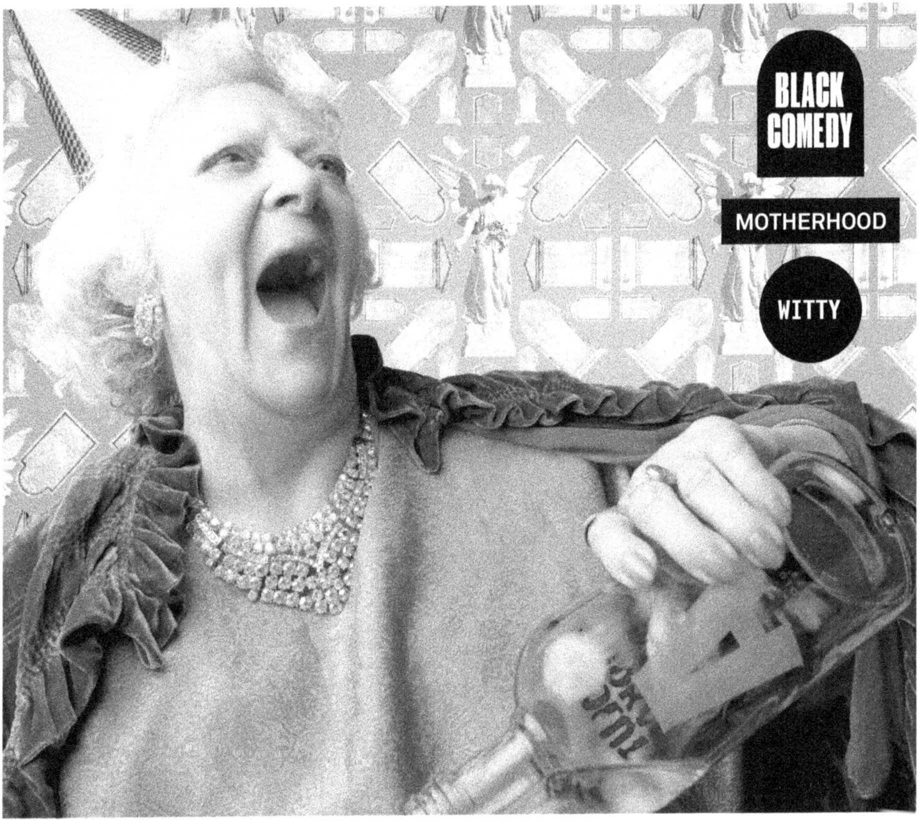

BLACK COMEDY

MOTHERHOOD

WITTY

GRIFFIN THEATRE COMPANY PRESENTS

GHOSTING THE PARTY

BY MELISSA BUBNIC

6 MAY – 11 JUNE 2022 | SBW STABLES THEATRE

DIRECTOR **ANDREA JAMES**
DESIGNER **ISABEL HUDSON**
LIGHTING DESIGNER **VERITY HAMPSON**
COMPOSER & SOUND DESIGNER **PHIL DOWNING**
STAGE MANAGER **MADELAINE OSBORN**

WITH
BELINDA GIBLIN
AMY HACK
JILLIAN O'DOWD

GRIFFIN THEATRE COMPANY

Government partners

Griffin acknowledges the generosity of the Seaborn, Broughton & Walford Foundation in allowing it the use of the SBW Stables Theatre rent free, less outgoings, since 1986.

PLAYWRIGHT'S NOTE

I'm scared of a premature death, dying young. And if I'm lucky enough to become old, I'm scared of my body and mind failing me... and not dying. Dying too soon and dying too late—both outcomes terrify me.

All my grandparents spent their final years in nursing homes suffering with dementia. You get to know the families of the other residents. And you almost always have the same conversation when you see them. Share war stories about your sick relative, bitch about the inadequacies of the nursing home, express guilt (for not doing more) and then helplessness (what more can anyone do?) and then agreeing that we'd all be better off dead than living like this.

I remember my mum telling me to 'shoot her in the head' if she ever got that bad. I know she didn't mean it literally. What my mum was saying is that she wants to avoid a bad end. I don't want to see my mum lose what makes her the person I know and love. And I don't want it to happen to me either.

But what is the alternative?

Maybe we'd be less scared of ageing if we had greater confidence that we would be well cared for. But the system repeatedly fails. There are the scandals of physical and sexual assaults that make national headlines, but also the hundreds of everyday incidents that are so routine they go unnoticed. Residents are forcibly restrained or isolated in locked rooms. Chemical restraint—where drugs are given to control behaviour rather than treat medical symptoms—is widespread. Residents develop chronic nappy rash due to sitting in wet undergarments for too long. Residents go hungry because they require assistance with eating and there's not enough staff. Residents are unwashed and their teeth unbrushed for weeks at a time. And so on, and so on.

Ghosting the Party is about three generations of women coming to terms with what it means to grow older, and what it means to be a mother, a daughter. The play asks uncomfortable questions about ageing, death, and familial obligation. It offers no answers. I have none.

You will die. Most of us don't know how or when. I hope to die in my sleep, an old woman, in otherwise reasonable health, satisfied that I lived a good, full life. But we so rarely get what we want.

Melissa Bubnic
Playwright

DIRECTOR'S NOTE

Ghosting the Party is a very special play that can make you laugh-gasp-laugh on your first read. From the moment Melissa playfully lists all the horrible ways you could die, I was hooked. And of course, we all want to know what happens in the end. Or do we? While we spend so much time avoiding death, how wonderfully refreshing is it to deeply consider this notion with humorous and womanly intent.

This seemingly never-ending pandemic has brought into sharp and tragic relief the delicate balance between life and death and (especially so) the plight of our elders in aged care homes. In the meantime, NSW Parliament has been fiercely debating a Voluntary Assisted Dying Bill that is being stalled in the upper house for all the wrong reasons. Melissa's deeply, darkly funny *Ghosting the Party* is definitely a play for these delicate and troublesome times.

Just when you think you're about to hunker down to a conventional micro-domestic intergenerational tragi-comedy... Melissa catapults us into a philosophical universe that asks us to contemplate death and domesticity throughout the ages. *Ghosting the Party* has an effortless knack of bringing the political into the intimately personal, while highlighting our boundless and universal capacity for caring—in all of its messy, hilarious and domestic reality.

At the age of 54, my mother, Sofia James, smoked her last cigarette, drank a coffee and took an intentional drug overdose underneath a blooming bottle brush tree in the backyard of my childhood home. Inside, the house was spotless, the bills were paid and there were no dishes or clothes left to wash. I wish my mother didn't have to die alone. I wish that society gave her something to live for. That she didn't feel like she'd been left on the scrap heap.

I wonder if this is what *Ghosting the Party* has to offer us? For it is a play about living, as much as it is about death.

And, while life and death can be so very, very hard, it can also be very beautiful.

Andrea James
Director

BIOGRAPHIES

MELISSA BUBNIC
WRITER

Melissa Bubnic is a writer for stage and screen. In 2011, Melissa completed a Masters in Writing for Performance at Goldsmiths, University of London. Her play *Beached* premiered at Melbourne Theatre Company and was staged at Griffin in 2013. *Beached* won the 2010 Patrick White Award from Sydney Theatre Company and was nominated for a Green Room Award in 2013. Melissa's play *Hedda*—an adaptation of *Hedda Gabler*—premiered at Queensland Theatre to universal acclaim in 2018. *Boys Will Be Boys*, starring Danielle Cormack and directed by Paige Rattray, was commissioned and premiered by Sydney Theatre Company in 2015 and has since been produced at London's Bush Theatre and Auckland's Silo Theatre Company. Her play, *Stop. Rewind* (directed by Anne Browning) premiered at Red Stitch Theatre in Melbourne in 2010 and toured Australia in 2012. Melissa's television credits include: for Disney Plus: *Nautilus*; for Sky Max: *A Town Called Malice*; and for Stan: *Two Hands*. She also has original projects in development with UK production companies Who's On First, New Pictures, Playground/BBC, Scott Free/Endeavor Content, and Carnival Films, and she is currently working on Australian projects with Hopscotch Features and Fremantle. Melissa won the Channel 4 Sonia Friedman Production Award for Best Play for *Monkey Work, Baboon Chop*. *Ghosting the Party* won The Lysicrates Prize in 2017.

ANDREA JAMES
DIRECTOR

Andrea is a Yorta Yorta/Gunaikurnai theatremaker and is a graduate of the Victorian College of the Arts. She was Artistic Director of Melbourne Workers Theatre from 2001–2008, where she is best known for her play *Yanagai! Yanagai!*. The play premiered at Playbox in 2004, was remounted in 2006 and toured to the UK. Andrea was the Aboriginal Arts Development Officer at Blacktown Arts Centre from 2010–2012 and was the Aboriginal Producer at Carriageworks from 2012–2016 before launching a career as a freelance theatremaker. She was recipient of British Council's Accelerate Program for Aboriginal Art Leaders in 2013 and was awarded the Create NSW Aboriginal Arts Fellowship in 2018. Andrea wrote and directed *Winyanboga Yurringa* at Carriageworks and Geelong Performing Arts Centre in 2016, and the play was remounted at Belvoir in 2019. Andrea's play *Sunshine Super Girl*, about Wiradjuri tennis star Evonne Goolagong-Cawley, premiered in Griffith in 2020, enjoyed a season at the 2021 Sydney Festival, and will embark on an extensive national tour in 2022. Her play *Dogged* was written with collaborator Catherine Ryan and premiered at Griffin in 2021. Andrea's current role as Griffin's Associate Artist complements her freelance practice as a playwright, director and dramaturg, where she continues to specialise in instigating and encouraging new First Nations plays with emerging and established artists nationwide.

ISABEL HUDSON
DESIGNER

Isabel is an award-winning set and costume designer. Isabel's design credits for the stage include: for Belvoir: *Every Brilliant Thing*, *Winyanboga Yurringa*; for Belvoir 25A: *Jess & Joe Forever*, *Tuesday*; for Bontom in association with Sydney Opera House, Edinburgh Festival, and a season in St Petersburg: *Chamber Pot Opera*; for Darlinghurst Theatre Company: *The Rise and Fall of Little Voice*; for Hayes Theatre Co: *Razorhurst, She Loves Me, The View Upstairs* (for which she received a Sydney Theatre Award nomination for Best Set Design of an Independent Production); for KXT bAKEHOUSE: *A Girl is a Half-Formed Thing, She Rode Horses Like the Stock Exchange, The Walworth Farce, You Got Older*; for Melbourne Theatre Company: *Torch the Place*; for NIDA: *Mr Burns*; for Outhouse Theatre Company in association with KXT bAKEHOUSE: *Dry Land* (for which she received a Sydney Theatre Award nomination for Best Set Design of an Independent Production); for Pinchgut Opera: *Farnace*; for Red Line Productions at the Old Fitz: *Eurydice, King of Pigs*; for Seymour Centre: *Blackrock, The Shifting Heart*; and for Sydney Festival 2021/Rising 2022: *Maureen: Harbinger of Death*. Isabel's set design credits include: for Hayes Theatre Co: *American Psycho, Cry-Baby, Young Frankenstein*. Isabel has won Sydney Theatre Awards for Best Set Design of an Independent Production two years in a row—for the musicals *American Psycho* and *Cry-Baby* at Hayes Theatre Co, which went on to tour to Sydney Opera House. Isabel is the Australian Set Associate for *Moulin Rouge! The Musical* (Global Creatures) and was recently awarded the Kristian Fredrikson Scholarship for Design. Isabel holds a Bachelor of Design from NIDA and a Bachelor of Arts (Screen and Sound) from the University of New South Wales.

VERITY HAMPSON
LIGHTING DESIGNER

Verity is a multi-award-winning lighting and projection designer who has designed over 130 productions, working with some of Australia's leading directors and choreographers. For theatre, Verity's designs include: for Griffin: *A Strategic Plan, And No More Shall We Part, Angela's Kitchen, Beached, Dealing With Clair, Dogged, Orange Thrower, The Bleeding Tree, The Boys, The Bull, The Moon and the Coronet of Stars, The Floating World, Superheroes, This Year's Ashes, The Turquoise Elephant*; for Griffin Independent: *The Brothers Size, The Cold Child, Crestfall, Family Stories: Belgrade, Live Acts On Stage, Music, The New Electric Ballroom, References to Salvador Dali Make Me Hot, Way to Heaven*; for Griffin and Bell Shakespeare: *The Literati*; for Bell Shakespeare: *A Midsummer Night's Dream, Julius Caesar, Titus Andronicus*; for Belvoir: *An Enemy of the People, The Drover's Wife, Faith Healer, Winyanboga Yurringa*; for CAAP/Sydney Festival: *Double Delicious*; for Dancenorth: *Dungarri Nya Nya Ngarri Bi Nya*; for Ensemble Theatre: *Baby Doll, Fully Committed*; for Hayes Theatre Co: *Lizzie*; for Malthouse Theatre: *Wake in Fright*; for Queensland Theatre: *Death of a Salesman*; and for Sydney Theatre Company: *7 Stages of Grieving, Blackie Blackie Brown, Grand Horizons, Hamlet: Prince of Skidmark, Home, I'm Darling, Machinal, Little Mercy*. Verity is a recipient of the Mike Walsh Fellowship; three Sydney Theatre Awards; a Green Room Award; and an APDG Award for Best Lighting Design.

PHIL DOWNING
COMPOSER & SOUND DESIGNER

Phil has been performing and recording music for over 20 years, and was first engaged to produce soundtracks for theatre through experimentation with original musical inventions. Phil's credits include: for Alice Osbourne/Performance Space: *Falling*; for Branch Nebula: *Artwork, Crush, High Performance Packing Tape, STOP-GO*; for Erth: *Murder*; for Moogahlin Performing Arts: *Rainbow's End, The Visitors, This Fella My Memory, Winyanboga Yurringa*; for My Darling Patricia: *Posts in the Paddock, The Piper*; for Side Pony Productions: *The Irresistible*; and for Vicky Van Hout: *Long Grass, Plenty Serious Talk Talk, Stolen*. Phil continues composing using various music recording/editing tools, creating sounds from found objects or manipulation of surroundings and the natural environment.

MADELAINE OSBORN
STAGE MANAGER

Madelaine is a theatremaker living and working primarily on Gadigal land as a stage manager, performer and producer. In 2015, she graduated from Charles Sturt University's B. Communication: Theatre/Media course with Distinction and was the 2015 recipient of the Blair Milan Memorial Scholarship. In 2015, she co-founded theatre collective Bite Productions as their resident producer and production manager. As stage manager, Madelaine's theatre credits include: for Griffin: Batch Festival, *Is There Something Wrong With That Lady?*; for Black Birds/Griffin: *Exhale*; for Australian Theatre for Young People: *Follow Me Home* (Riverside Theatres 2019 Season and 2021 Tour), *INTERSECTION: Arrival*; for Bondi Feast: *MARS: An Interplanetary Cabaret*; and as assistant stage manager: for Performing Lines: *Sunshine Super Girl* (Development and Tour). Additional producing credits include: for Little Eggs/KXT bAKEHOUSE: *Symphonie Fantastique*; for sandpaperplane/Old 505: *Pit*. Madelaine is particularly passionate about creating new Australian work that is accessible and empowering to minority groups and communities that may not regularly be exposed to theatre and performance art. She is delighted to be returning to the SBW Stables Theatre this year.

AMY HACK
SUZIE

Amy Hack is a graduate of Actors Centre Australia, Atlantic Theatre Company (NYC), and Patrick Studios Australia's dance and professional development course. Amy's theatre credits include: for Griffin: *A is for Apple, First Love is the Revolution* (for which she received a Sydney Theatre Award nomination for Best Supporting Actor), *Shabbat Dinner*; for Bell Shakespeare (The Players): *Romeo & Juliet*; for Hayes Theatre Co: *American Psycho, Caroline, or Change* (for which she received a Sydney Theatre Award nomination for Best Supporting Actor), *Cry-Baby, Young Frankenstein*; for One Eyed Man Productions: *Spamalot* (National Tour); for KXT bAKEHOUSE: *Wrath*; for Red Line Productions at the Old Fitz: *Amongst Ruins*; for La Mama Theatre: *Intoxication*; for SheShakespeare: *As You Like It*. Amy's film and television credits include: *After the Verdict, The Secret She Keeps, Amazing Grace, Brock, Hyde & Seek*, and the independent films *Infinite Shades of Grey, Equivocal Resolve, Periphery* and *Orgy*. Amy is a proud resident actor with the Ignite Collective and has worked as movement director & choreographer on various music videos for artists including Belinda Woods and Don the Toga.

BELINDA GIBLIN
GRACE

Belinda is one of Australia's most distinguished stage and screen actors. Her theatre credits include: for Griffin: *Family Values, Love Child* (which she also produced), *The Turquoise Elephant, Wicked Sisters*; for Adrian Bohm: *The Vagina Monologues*; for Apocalypse Theatre Company and Red Line Productions at the Old Fitz: *Doubt* (for which she was nominated for a Sydney Theatre Award); for Red Line Productions at the Old Fitz: *Happy Days* (for which she was nominated for a Sydney Theatre Award); for Christine Dunstan Productions: *The Shoehorn Sonata*; for Christine Dunstan Productions and Company B: *Scam*; for Darlinghurst Theatre Company: *Daylight Saving*; for Ensemble Theatre: *Absurd Person Singular, Dark Voyager, Noises Off*; for Gary Penny Productions: *Steaming*; for Marian Street Theatre: *Canaries Sometimes Sing, Henceforward, How the Other Half Lives, Social Climbers, Things We Do For Love*; for Melbourne Theatre Company, Red Line Productions at the Old Fitz, Strange Duck Productions and Sydney Opera House: *Blonde Poison* (for which she was nominated for a Sydney Theatre Award); for Outhouse Theatre: *John* (for which she was nominated for a Sydney Theatre Award); for Perth Theatre Company: *Same Time Another Year*; for Playbox Theatre: *Quadraphenia, The World is Made of Glass*; for Queensland Theatre: *Blithe Spirit*; for Sport for Jove: *Ear to the Edge of Time*; and for Sydney Theatre Company: *Away*. Belinda's film credits include: *A Stitch in Time, The Box, Demolition, The Empty Beach, Endplay, On the Edge of the Bed, Peterson, Say You Want Me* (for which she won a Sammy Award) and an award-winning short film *Stille Nacht*. In 2021, she featured as Elizabeth 1 in the Sport for Jove/Soap Productions film: *Venus and Adonis*. Her television credits include: for ABC: *MDA*; for Network Ten: *The Box, Heartbreak High*; for Nine Network: *Good Guys Bad Guys, The Sullivans*; and for Seven Network: *A Country Practice, Home and Away, Skyways, Sons and Daughters*.

JILLIAN O'DOWD
DOROTHY

Jillian is a Kiwi-born, Bachelor of Dramatic Arts NIDA graduate of 1996. Jilly's voice credits include: for ABC Illawarra Radio: *PIP!*; for ABC Kids: *Guess How Much I Love You*; and for Trackdown Studios: *Nate is Late*. Jilly has performed roles for Belvoir, Bell Shakespeare, Sydney Theatre Company, and internationally for TNT British Theatre and Traffic of the Stage (UK). Other theatre credits include: for The Comedy Co. (UK); *Dinnerladies*; for The ARTSLAB: *Safety Nets*; for First Night Productions: *The Witches of Eastwick*; and *Hugh Jackman: The Boy from Oz* (National Arena Tour). Jillian's TV credits include: for ABC: *Come in Spinner*, *Love is a Four Letter Word*, *Rake*; for ITV (UK): *Cold Feet*; for Nine Network: *The Girl From Tomorrow*, *Water Rats*; for Seven Network: *A Country Practice, All Saints, Home and Away, Sixpack*; and the recent Arena media web series *The Five Minute Call*. Her film credits include: *Dead Letter Office*, *Diana Clone, The Flood, Small Claims, The Three Stooges* and *Walking on Water*. Jilly was a training and development consultant, director, and teacher at the London School of Dramatic Art and is the Education Director for TPAC. Jilly plays drums and sings with singer-songwriter Baxter Stone, and also directs and produces their music videos and *Sweet Beats 'n' Blues* events. Jilly is in creative development with poet/artist Greer Taylor for a multimedia event, *Veiling:grief and delight*. Jilly appreciates being a part of telling Melissa's bold new Australian story on Gadigal country for Griffin.

ABOUT GRIFFIN

Griffin is the only theatre company in the country exclusively devoted to the development and staging of new Australian writing. Located in the historic SBW Stables Theatre, nestled in the heart of Kings Cross, Griffin has been Australia's home for the exploration of new stories since 1978.

We are the launch pad for new plays, ideas and writing that other theatres won't take a risk on. We boldly contribute to Australia's unique and powerful storytelling culture. Plays like *Prima Facie*, *Holding the Man* and *City of Gold* all had their world premieres at Griffin before going out to capture the national imagination. In the words of our longest-serving Artistic Director, **Ros Horin:**

"We are the theatre of first chances."

We are passionate about nurturing emerging and established practitioners alike. We pride ourselves on supporting our vast community of artists, audiences and supporters who consider our theatre their creative home. We help ambitious, bold, risk-taking and urgent Australian work get from the page onto the stage. We tell the stories that help us know who we are as a nation, and who we want to become.

Acknowledgement of Country

Griffin Theatre Company and the SBW Stables Theatre operate and tell stories on the unceded lands of the Gadigal of the Eora Nation. We acknowledge and honour Aboriginal and Torres Strait Islander people as the oldest continuous living culture on the planet, with more than 60,000 years of storytelling practice shaping and underpinning all aspects of Australian culture. It is a privilege that we do not take lightly: to work on this land, and to tell stories on its soil.

GRIFFIN THEATRE COMPANY
13 Craigend St
Kings Cross NSW 2011

02 9332 1052
info@griffintheatre.com.au
griffintheatre.com.au

SBW STABLES THEATRE
10 Nimrod St
Kings Cross NSW 2011

BOOKINGS
griffintheatre.com.au
02 9361 3817

GRIFFIN FAMILY

Patron
Seaborn, Broughton & Walford Foundation

Griffin acknowledges the generosity of the Seaborn, Broughton & Walford Foundation in allowing it the use of the SBW Stables Theatre rent free, less outgoings, since 1986.

Board
Bruce Meagher (Chair)
Guillaume Babille
Simon Burke AO
Helen Dai
Lyndell Droga
Tim Duggan
Declan Greene
Julia Pincus
Lenore Robertson
Simone Whetton

Artistic Director & CEO
Declan Greene

Executive Director & CEO
Julieanne Campbell

Associate Artistic Director
Tessa Leong

Associate Artist
Andrea James

Literary Associate
Julian Larnach

Box Office Manager
Dominic Scarf

Bar Manager
Alex Bryant-Smith

Front of House
Bridget Haberecht, Julian Larnach, Poppy Tidswell, Jackson Used

Associate Producer, Development
Frankie Greene

Development Coordinator
Ell Katte

Finance Manager
Kylie Richards

Finance Consultant
Emma Murphy

Marketing Manager (Acting)
Ang Collins

Marketing Coordinator
Sasha Meaney

Production Manager
Jeremy Page

Production Coordinator
Ally Moon

Senior Producer
Imogen Gardam

Programs Producer
Janine Lau

Ticketing & Administration Coordinator
Kate Marks

Strategic Insights Consultant
Peter O'Connell

Sustainability Coordinators
Ang Collins, Julian Larnach

Brand & Graphic Design
Alphabet

Web Developer
DevQuoll

Cover Photography
Brett Boardman

GRIFFIN DONORS

Income from Griffin activities covers less than 40% of our operating costs—leaving an ever-increasing gap for us to fill through government funding, sponsorship and the generosity of our individual supporters. Your support helps us bridge the gap and keep ticket prices affordable and our work at its best. To make a donation and a difference, contact Griffin on **9332 1052** or donate online at **griffintheatre.com.au**

PROGRAM PATRONS

Griffin Ambassadors
Robertson Foundation

Griffin Amplify
Girgensohn Foundation

Griffin Studio
Gil Appleton
Darin Cooper Foundation
Kiong Lee & Richard Funston
Rosemary Hannah &
Lynette Preston
Ken & Lilian Horler
Malcolm Robertson Foundation
Pip Rath & Wayne Lonergan
Geoff &
Wendy Simpson OAM
Danielle Smith &
Sean Carmody
Walking up the Hill Foundation

Griffin Studio Workshop
Mary Ann Rolfe (Patron)
Darin Cooper Foundation
Bob Ernst
Susan MacKinnon
Pip Rath & Wayne Lonergan

Griffin Women's Initiative
Anonymous (1)
Katrina Barter
Wendy Blacklock
Christy Boyce & Madeleine Beaumont
Julieanne Campbell
Iolanda Capodanno
Laura Crennan
Jennifer Darin
Lyndell Droga
Melinda Graham
Sherry Gregory
Rosemary Hannah &
Lynette Preston
Antonia Haralambis
Ann Johnson
Roanne Knox
Susan MacKinnon
Julia Pincus
Ruth Ritchie
Lenore Robertson
Sonia Simich
Deanne Weir
Simone Whetton

Griffin Women's Initiative was originally supported by Creative Partnerships Australia through Plus1

SEASON PATRONS

As a new writing theatre, we program a wide range of stories that reflect our time, place and the unique voice of contemporary Australia. To ensure that these stories continue to be told, Griffin needs the help of private support to bring strength, insight, candour and new and powerful visions to the stage. Our Production Partner program is vital to our continued artistic success.

PRODUCTION PARTNERS 2022

Whitefella Yella Tree by Dylan Van Den Berg
Darin Cooper Foundation
Richard McHugh &
Kate Morgan

PRODUCTION PARTNERS 2021

***Dogged* by Andrea James & Catherine Ryan**
Lisa Barker & Don Russell
Darin Cooper Foundation
Robert Dick & Erin Shiel
Lyndell & Daniel Droga
Danny Gilbert AM &
Kathleen Gilbert
Rosemary Hannah &
Lynette Preston
Bruce Meagher &
Greg Waters
Richard McHugh &
Kate Morgan
Julia Pincus &
Ian Learmonth
Pip Rath & Wayne Lonergan

SEASON DONORS

Company Patron $100,000+
Neilson Foundation

Season Patron $50,000+
Girgensohn Foundation
Robertson Foundation

Mainstage Donors $20,000+
Darin Cooper Foundation
Robert Dick & Erin Shiel
Rosemary Hannah & Lynette Preston
Julia Pincus & Ian Learmonth
Mary Ann Rolfe

Production Donors $10,000+
Anonymous (1)
Lisa Barker & Don Russell
Gordon & Marie Esden
Abraham & Helen James

GRIFFIN DONORS

Ingrid Kaiser
Richard McHugh &
Kate Morgan
Bruce Meagher &
Greg Waters
Peter & Dianne O'Connell
Pip Rath & Wayne Lonergan
The WeirAnderson
Foundation
Kim Williams AM &
Catherine Dovey

**Rehearsal Donors
$5,000 - $9,999**
Anonymous (1)
Antoinette Albert
Gil Appleton
Wendy Blacklock
Ellen Borda
Susan Carleton
Bernard Coles
Ian Dickson
Lyndell & Daniel Droga
Danny Gilbert AM &
Kathleen Gilbert
Ken & Lilian Horler
Lambert Bridge Foundation
Kiong Lee & Richard Funston
Lee Lewis & Brett Boardman
Sophie McCarthy &
Antony Green
Catriona Morgan-Hunn
Anthony Paull
Rebel Penfold-Russell OAM
Geoff & Wendy Simpson OAM
The Sky Foundation
Merilyn Sleigh &
Raoul de Ferranti
Danielle Smith &
Sean Carmody
Walking Up the Hill
Foundation

**Final Draft Donors
$3,000-$4,999**
Jocelyn Goyen
Sherry Gregory
James Hartwright &
Kerrin D'Arcy
Roanne & John Knox
Don & Leslie Parsonage
Leslie Stern

**Workshop Donors
$1,000-$2,999**
Anonymous (4)
Baly Douglass Foundation
Katrina Barter
Helen Bauer &
Helen Lynch AM
Cherry & Peter Best
Christy Boyce &
Madeleine Beaumont
Dr Bernadette Brennan
Anne Britton
Corinne & Bryan
Stephen & Annabelle Burley
Julieanne Campbell
Iolanda Capodanno
Louise Christie
Anna Cleary
Bryony & Tim Cox
Sally Crawford
Laura Crennan
Cris Croker & David West
Bob Ernst
Ros & Paul Espie
Brian Everingham
Jan Ewert
John & Libby Fairfax
Sandra Forbes
Jennifer Giles
Nicky Gluyas
Melinda Graham
Peter Gray & Helen Thwaites
Antonia Haralambis
Kate Harrison
John Head
Libby Higgin
Mark Hopkinson &
Michelle Opie
Michael Jackson
Ann Johnson
David & Adrienne Kitching
Elizabeth Laverty
Benjamin Law
Richard & Elizabeth Longes
Kyrsty Macdonald &
Christopher Hazell
Susan MacKinnon
Prudence Manrique
Lorin Muhlmann
Jane Munro
David Nguyen
Ian Phipps
Martin Portus
Annabel Ritchie
In memory of
Katherine Robertson
Sylvia Rosenblum
Sonia Simich
Jann Skinner
Stuart Thomas
Elizabeth Thompson
Mike Thompson
Sue Thomson
Janet Wahlquist
Richard Weinstein &
Richard Benedict
Simone Whetton
Rob White & Lisa Hamilton
Rosemary White
Paul & Jennifer Winch
Elizabeth Wing

Reading Donors $500-$999
Anonymous (3)
Brian Abel
Priscilla Adey
Jane Albert
Amity Alexander
Wendy Ashton
Robyn Ayres
Melissa Ball
Phillip Black
Larry Boyd &
Barbara Caine AM
Tim Capelin
Michael Diamond AM MBE
Max Dingle OAM
Elizabeth Diprose
David Earp
Leonie Flannery
Alan Froude & David Round
Peter Graves

GRIFFIN DONORS

Erica Gray
Stephanie & Andrew Harrison
David Hoskins & Paul McKnight
Sylvia Hrovatin
Nicki Jam
Mira Joksovic
Matt Jones & Rebecca Bourne Jones
Colleen Mary Kane
Susan J Kath
Patricia Lynch
Ian & Elizabeth MacDonald
Suzanne & Anthony Maple-Brown
Robert Marks
Chris Marrable & Kate Richardson
Simon Marrable & Anna Kasper
Christopher Matthies
Christopher McCabe
John McCallum & Jenny Nicholls
Daniela McMurdo
Jacqui Mercer
John Mitchell
Neville Mitchell
Keith Moynihan
Patricia Novikoff
Carolyn Penfold
Belinda Piggott & David Ojerholm
Virginia Pursell
Alex-Oonagh Redmond
Karen Rodgers & Bill Harris
Gemma Rygate
Rob & Rae Spence
Mary Stollery & Eric Dole
Catherine Sullivan & Alexandra Bowen
Ariadne Vromen
Robyn Fortescue & Rosie Wagstaff
Helen Wicker

First Draft Donors $200-$499
Anonymous (10)
Susan Ambler
Elizabeth Antonievich
William Armitage
Chris Baker
Jan Barr
John Bell AO, OBE
Edwina Birch
Andrew Bowmer
Peter Brown
Wendy Buswell
Ruth Campbell
David Caulfield
Amanda Clark
Sue Clark
Louise Costanzo
Brendan Crotty & Darryl Toohey
Bryan Cutler
Sue Donnelly
Peter Duerden
Anna Duggan
Kathy Esson
Elizabeth Evatt
Michael Eyers
Helen Ford
Judith Fox
Eva Gerber
Jock Given
Deane Golding
Keith Gow
Virginia & Kieran Greene
Jo Grisard
Edwina Guinness
Ruth Guss
Kate Haddock
Raewyn Harlock
Robert Henderson & Marijke Conrade
Grania Hickley
Matthew Huxtable
Marian & Nabeel Ibrahim
Andrew Inglis
James Landon-Smith
Penelope Latey
Liz Locke

Danielle Long
Norman Long
Noella Lopez
Maruschka Loupis
Anni MacDougall
Claire McCaughan
Louise McDonald
Duncan McKay
Paula McLean
Stephen McNamara
Anne Miehs
Julia Mitchell
Mark Mitchell
Sarah Mort
Margaret Murphy
Carolyn Newman
Suzanne Osmond
Catherine & Joshua Palmer
Peter Pezzutti
Christopher Powell
Janelle Prescott
Andrew Pringle
Dorothy & Adit Rao
Tracey Robson
Ann Rocca
Catherine Rothery
Kevin and Shirley Ryan
Dimity Scales
Julia Selby
Natalie Shea
Vivienne Skinner
Bridget Smith
Vanda and Martin Smith
Augusta Supple
Danny Tomic
Rachel Trigg
Samantha Turley
Adam Van Rooijen
Julie Whitfield
Eve Wynhausen
Robert Yuen
William Zappa

We would also like to thank Peter O'Connell for his expertise, guidance, and time.

Current as of 21 March 2022

SPONSORS

Griffin would like to thank the following:

OUR PARTNERS

Government Supporters

Benefactor

Creative Partners

  GIRGENSOHN FOUNDATION

Company Sponsors

Griffin Theatre Company is assisted by the Australian Government through the Australia Council, its arts funding and advisory body; and the NSW Government through Create NSW.

www.ingramcontent.com/pod-product-compliance
Lightning Source LLC
Chambersburg PA
CBHW050026090426
42734CB00021B/3438